THE HOLOCAUST

Resistance to the Nazis

Jane Shuter

Heinemann Library
Chicago, Illinois

© 2003 Reed Educational & Professional Publishing
Published by Heinemann Library,
an imprint of Reed Educational & Professional Publishing,
Chicago, Illinois

Customer Service 888-454-2279

Visit our website at www.heinemannlibrary.com

Designed by Joanna Sapwell and Tinstar Design
Illustrations by Martin Griffin
Originated by Ambassador Litho Ltd
Printed in Hong Kong, by Wing
King Tong

07 06 05 04 03
10 9 8 7 6 5 4 3 2 1

Library of Congress
Cataloging-in-Publication Data
Shuter, Jane.
  Resistance to the Nazis / Jane Shuter.
    p. cm. -- (The Holocaust)
Summary: Describes how certain people, both Jews and
Gentiles, were
brave enough to stand up to the Nazis during the
Holocaust despite the
price they would pay if caught.
Includes bibliographical references and index.
  ISBN 1-4034-0814-9 (HC), 1-4034-3206-6 (Pbk.)
  1. Germany--History--1933-1945--Juvenile literature. 2.
Holocaust,
Jewish (1939-1945)--Juvenile literature. 3. Anti-Nazi
movement--Europe--Juvenile literature. [1. Germany--
History--1933-1945.
2. Holocaust, Jewish (1939-1945) 3. Righteous Gentiles in
the Holocaust.
4. World War, 1939-1945--Jewish resistance. 5. World War,
1939-1945--Jews--Rescue.] I. Title. II. Holocaust (Chicago,
Ill.)
  DD256.3 .S5 2003
  943.086--dc21
                    2002006853

Acknowledgments
The author and publisher are grateful to the following for
permission to reproduce copyright material: p. 6 SCR; p. 7
Tomi Ungerer & Diogense Verlag Ag Zurich; p. 8 Imperial
War Museum; pp. 9, 39 Ullstein Bilderdienst; pp. 10, 34, 45
Popperfoto; pp. 11, 12, 13, 15, 32, 43, 46, 47 USHMM; pp.
16, 17, 21, 22, 23, 42 Auschwitz-Birkenau State Museum; p.
19 Mittelbau-Dora/M. De La Pintiere; pp. 20a, 20b Emma
Robertson & Magnet Harlequin; p. 24 Ronald Grant
Archive; p. 26 Meczenstwo Walka, Zaglada Zydów Polsce
1939-1945. Poland. No. 80.; p. 27 Irene Gut Opdyke; p. 28
Corbis; pp. 29, 31, 37, 48 Hulton Archive; p. 30 Eva Maria
Elfes; pp. 33, 44 Yad Vashem; p. 35 Robert Hunt Library; p.
36 Bilderdienst Suddeutscher Verlag; p. 38 Yivo Institute;
pp. 40, 49 Mary Evans Picture Library; p. 41 AKG.

Cover photograph shows a group of Lithuanian partisans
in July 1944, reproduced with permission of
USHMM/ITAR-TASS.

Special thanks to Ronald Smelser and Sally Brown-Winter.

About the series consultants
Ronald Smelser is a history professor at the University
of Utah. He has written or edited eight books on the
Holocaust and over three dozen articles. His recent
publications include *Learning About the Holocaust: A Student
Guide* (4 vol.) and *Lessons and Legacies: The Holocaust and
Justice*. Professor Smelser is also a past president of the
German Studies Association.

Sally Brown-Winter has worked in the field of Jewish
Education as a principal and teacher for over 25 years.
In her schools, the Shoah—its history, lessons, and
implications—have been explored from kindergarten
through high school.

Some words are shown in bold, **like this.** You can find out what they mean by looking
in the glossary.

Contents

Resistance to the Holocaust

In 1933 the **Nazis,** led by Adolf Hitler, became the ruling party in Germany. The Nazis wanted to create a new German empire that they called the **Third Reich.** Gradually, Germany began to take control of other lands, including Austria and part of Czechoslovakia in 1938. When Germany invaded Poland in early September 1939, Britain and France declared war on Germany. World War II had begun.

During the first years of the war, German forces swept through Europe. The Nazis took over other countries and forced the people living in them to obey Nazi rules. Sometimes they allowed the government of a country to go on ruling that country—as long as it did so the Nazi way. Sometimes Nazi officials were sent to run a country, with a German army and police system to keep control.

German Expansion, 1933–1941

This map shows how Germany took over more and more countries between 1933 and the end of 1941. The Nazis tried to enforce their ideas in the countries they **occupied.**

borders in 1933
extent of German occupation
Germany in 1933
Germany by end of 1938
Germany by end of 1939
Germany by end of 1940
Germany by end of 1941
Countries controlled by or allied to Germany by end of 1941

NORWAY
FINLAND
SWEDEN
ESTONIA
DENMARK
LATVIA
LITHUANIA
EAST PRUSSIA
GREAT BRITAIN
EIRE (IRELAND)
THE NETHERLANDS
SOVIET UNION
GERMANY
BELGIUM
POLAND
FRANCE
CZECHOSLOVAKIA
BESSARABIA
SWITZERLAND
AUSTRIA
"VICHY" FRANCE
HUNGARY
ROMANIA
YUGOSLAVIA
ITALY
BULGARIA
PORTUGAL
SPAIN
ALBANIA
GREECE
TURKEY
AFRICA
SYRIA

Moving Toward the Holocaust

Among the things the Nazis demanded was that their **anti-Semitic** policies against **Jewish** people should be carried out in the countries they took over. They insisted that lists be made of all of the Jews living in the country. These lists gave the names, addresses, and occupations of everyone in each Jewish family. This information made it easier for the Nazis to find these people when they moved to the next stage—removing the Jews' rights to work and be treated equally with non-Jewish people. After taking away Jewish people's rights, the Nazis moved them into **transit camps.** There they lived in terrible conditions until they were transferred to camps where they were used as slave labor or to camps where they were murdered. The Nazis' attempt to murder all of the Jewish people in the lands they controlled is called the **Holocaust.** It has been calculated that the Nazis killed nearly six million Jews before they were defeated in 1945. The end of World War II in Europe stopped the Holocaust.

Resisting the Nazis

This book is mainly about the people who resisted the Nazis' treatment of Jews and the Holocaust. We will see how these people resisted and how much people actually knew about the Holocaust. However, there was also resistance to the Nazis for reasons other than their treatment of Jews. Many people in the countries taken over by the Nazis set up resistance groups to fight the Nazis and drive them out of their countries.

What Did They Know?

Once World War II ended, the truth about the Holocaust began to emerge. Over the years since then, many people have researched the Holocaust. We know far more about it now than people did at the time. While the Holocaust was going on, people knew that the Nazis had built many **concentration camps** and **labor camps** where people who opposed the Nazis were sent. They also knew that the Nazis were anti-Semitic and were persecuting Jewish people. However, the Nazis were careful not to talk openly about the Holocaust. There were rumors about what happened to the many trainloads of Jewish people who were sent east to Poland to be **"resettled."** But, the idea that the Nazis were committing mass murder of these people was very hard to believe, even when evidence began to emerge. At the time, it seemed unbelievable that anyone could behave in this way towards innocent men, women, and children.

The Jewish People

Many **Jews** and others who lived in lands **occupied** by the **Nazis** did not resist Nazi persecution of the Jews. Why not?

- Some people supported the Nazis. There were **anti-Semitic** groups in some countries, such as France and Hungary, who actively helped the Nazis to identify Jewish people.

- Some people hoped that things would stop getting worse and begin to get better. This was true even of Jewish people in terrible conditions. We know, now that it is over, what happened in the **Holocaust.** Most of the people who were murdered did not realize what was going to happen until it was too late.

- Many Jewish people were in a poor position to resist. They had few or no weapons or other supplies to fight. They knew the Nazis would execute many people from their community if they resisted and failed. Even escaping was a problem—many people had elderly relatives who were too frail to go.

- Many non-Jewish people were too frightened, for themselves and their families and friends, to help Jews or to resist the Nazis. They knew that anyone caught resisting would be hanged, shot, or sent to the **camps.** Often the Nazis killed a hundred or more people for one German soldier shot by resistance groups.

Nazi "Justice"

Irene Gut Opdyke, who was a nurse in Radom when the Germans invaded Poland, remembers: "'Whoever helps a Jew will be punished by death' was the warning that was repeated on posters and loudspeakers on the street."

The Nazis made sure people knew these threats were real by staging public hangings, like this one of some Russian **partisans.** Irene, who was herself hiding Jews, saw Nazi "justice" in action:

> One day I walked into the crowded square to find I could not pass through. A Polish couple and two small children were pushed up onto a small platform and behind them another couple with a toddler, with yellow stars on their coats. Their crimes were announced. The Jews were enemies of the **Reich;** the Poles had been harboring them. For the Jews, a sentence of death was the law. For the Poles, the punishment for helping a Jew was also death. No trial. No mercy. It took no time to hang them. No time at all.

ROBERT LOURSON
ICI LONDRES!
LA B.B.C. PENDANT LA GUERRE

Listening to the Radio

In all of the countries controlled by the Nazis, including Germany itself, it was illegal to listen to any radio broadcasts except those broadcast by Nazi-approved radio stations. One of the most common kinds of resistance to the Nazis during the war was disobeying this rule. People listened to British or U.S. broadcasts with the volume turned down very low. The punishment for this small resistance was anything from five years in prison to execution.

Different Kinds of Resistance

Many people did fight or try to prevent the Nazis from killing the Jews and other people. They resisted the Nazis in different ways, depending on their circumstances. People starving in **concentration camps** did not have the same chance to resist as free people in occupied countries.

People who managed to escape from Nazi-controlled countries could join the **Allies** and fight the Nazis quite openly. In occupied countries, people had to be more careful about how they resisted. Many people acted as though they accepted Nazi rule while secretly helping Jews to escape, **sabotaging** Nazi troops, or passing on information about the Nazis to the Allies.

People who were prisoners of the Nazis, in camps or **ghettos,** were seldom able to physically fight them, although they did so at times. They resisted constantly in other ways, though. For example, ghettos were areas of Polish cities that Jews were forced to move into—they were the only places Jews were allowed to live. In most ghettos, schools were banned, yet people carried on teaching children in secret. They refused to let the Nazis stop them from passing on their knowledge, culture, and skills. The Nazis banned religious services of any kind, Jewish or non-Jewish, in their prisons and **labor camps,** but people still held these services in secret, despite the fact that they would be executed if caught.

Fighting the Nazis

Some **Jewish** people got far enough away from Germany, fast enough, to be able to fight the **Nazis** with the **Allies** during World War II. They joined many other Jewish people already living in these countries who wanted to fight the Nazis.

World War II broke out in 1939 and various countries fought Germany at different times. Jewish people who got out of Germany and joined the Allies fought the Nazis in many different ways. They fought in the armed forces or worked in army hospitals. They helped to break Nazi codes and even went back into German-**occupied** land to organize resistance there. As the German army advanced over Europe, more people from occupied countries joined the fight against Nazi control.

In 1940, the British set up the Special Operations Executive, **SOE,** to cause as much trouble in occupied Europe as possible—"to set Europe ablaze," as the British Prime Minister, Winston Churchill, said. Many **refugees** from Hitler's Europe joined the SOE, and some of them were Jewish.

Where Did They Fight?

Jewish people fought with the Russian, Polish, French, British, and U.S. armed forces—wherever they were fighting. Jews from Canada, Australia, and New Zealand also fought. Palestinian Jews fought in Greece, North Africa, and Italy. Thirty-two Palestinian Jews were parachuted into German-controlled land to help the **partisans** and try to set up escape lines for Jewish people. Seven of them, including two women, were caught by the Germans and executed.

Prayers for the Soldiers

In 1944, a Jewish Brigade was formed in the British army. The people in it wore a Star of David along with the usual army badges. These Jewish soldiers were sent to fight the German army in North Africa. There were so many Jewish people in the various British armed forces that a special *Prayer Book for Jewish Members of the Armed Forces* was printed in 1940. It had specially written prayers for going into battle and for the sick and wounded, as well as traditional Hebrew prayers.

Enigma

Some of the hardest and most important information to get in a war is information about what the enemy plans to do. The Germans sent messages to each other using radio transmitters. The Allies could pick up these messages, but they were in a complicated code that was worked out on a machine (shown here) that the British nicknamed "Enigma." The first steps to cracking the code came when Polish escapees managed to bring parts of one of these machines to Britain. Scientists figured out how the machine worked, but it was impossible to guess the words needed to set the machine. Then a codebook was found after a battle at sea. Until the codebook became out of date, the Allies were able to break the code and know what the Germans were going to do next.

New Ideas

Some refugees who escaped to Britain in the early 1930s were scientists who helped develop weapons and equipment such as radar. They brought new ideas and ways of thinking out of Germany. Medical researchers were also important. Ernst Chain was a refugee from Germany who helped turn penicillin into a usable antibiotic. This new drug saved thousands of lives in the war.

An Added Danger

Jews who fought the Germans faced more brutal treatment than others if they were caught. The treatment of prisoners-of-war (soldiers captured in war) was set by rules drawn up in Switzerland in 1865.

This set of rules was called the Geneva Convention. The Nazis applied these rules to some prisoners and not to others. Prisoners from Britain, Scandinavia, or the U.S. were more likely to be treated properly.

Nazi ideas about **race** led them to see these prisoners-of-war as coming from the same **Aryan** race as Germans. On the other hand, captured Russian soldiers or Jews from any country were more likely to be treated badly. The Nazis thought they were from inferior races. Jewish prisoners-of-war were separated from the people they were captured with and sent to **concentration camps.**

Undercover in France

Peter Deman was living in Vienna when the **Nazis** took over Austria. He decided at once that **Jews** were better off out of Austria and emigrated to France. He could speak fluent French, English, and German. He joined the French army and fought until he was captured by the Germans in 1940. He was put into a prisoner-of-war camp as a French soldier—the Nazis had not realized that he was Jewish. Deman escaped from the camp and joined the **Foreign Legion** as a way to escape Nazi rule. As soon as he was outside land controlled by Germany, he deserted from the Foreign Legion and went to Britain. There he was welcomed for his experience and language skills and became a member of **SOE,** the Special Operations Executive.

In the fall of 1943, Deman went back to France as an SOE agent based in Rennes. The SOE had provided him with **papers** that showed he was an insurance salesman who was excused from military service because he had a weak heart. He found himself a base on the coast and began smuggling people and equipment in and out from several local beaches. One of these beaches was just 39 feet (12 meters) from a German lookout. The German officer in charge cooperated with Deman and his men. In the words of one of Deman's helpers: "He took care not to look."

In the summer of 1944, Deman's route was moving, on average, seven people a week out of France under the noses of the Germans.

Resistance in France

The French resistance did not have the weapons, supplies, or training to fight the German army in open battle. They fought by **sabotaging** road and railroad links and ambushing groups of Nazis, using well-trained gunmen like the resistance fighter shown here.

Hannah Senesh's Last Poem

Hannah Senesh wrote poetry. This is her last poem, written in prison:

One-Two-Three

One-two-three . . . eight feet long,
Two strides across, the rest is dark . . .
Life hangs over me like a question mark.

One-two-three . . . maybe another week,
Or next month may still find me here,
But death, I feel, is very near.

I could have been twenty-three next July;
I gambled on what matters most,
The dice were thrown. I lost.

Hannah Senesh

Hannah Senesh was born in Hungary in 1921. She went to live in Palestine in September 1939. In August 1942, a group of Polish women arrived in Palestine. They told of the **death camps** and conditions in the **concentration camps.** A group of Palestinians decided to parachute into Yugoslavia to try to get as many Jews out of lands **occupied** by Germany as possible. Hannah was one of them. The British—who controlled Palestine at this time—trained them and made them British officers. In exchange, they had to try to free **Allied** pilots in prisoner-of-war camps. The parachutists left from Brindisi, Italy, on March 13, 1944. Hannah crossed into Hungary on June 7, 1944.

Hannah said:

We are the only ones who can help; we don't have the right to think of our own safety, we don't have the right to hesitate. Even if there is only a slight chance of success, we must go. If we don't go, for fear of our lives, a million Jews will be massacred. If we succeed, we can open up an escape route that will save millions.

The Nazis caught seven of the parachutists, including Hannah. While in prison she met another parachutist, Yoel Palgi, and told him how she was captured. On October 28, 1944, she was tried for the "crime" of coming to save Jewish people. She admitted it and boldly spoke against Nazi policy. The Hungarian judges delayed sentencing her until November 4, hoping the Americans or Russians would arrive. The Nazis executed her on November 7, 1944.

Resistance in the Ghettos

Resistance was harder in lands controlled by Germany, especially for **Jewish** people. From 1939, the **Nazis** shut Jewish people up in **ghettos**—walled-off areas of big cities. The ghettos left the rest of the German-**occupied** lands free of Jews. Did being put together help Jewish people to resist? Living conditions in the ghetto were hard. People had to struggle daily to work, find enough food to live, obey the Nazis' rules, and avoid Nazi round-ups. The Nazis used **informers** in the ghettos and privacy was hard to find. New people arrived and others were taken away, almost daily. Trusting anyone enough to plan resistance of any kind was nearly impossible.

Education

Each ghetto was run by a *Judenrat* (Jewish Council) that carried out Nazi orders. The Nazis did not allow schools in most ghettos. Despite this, parents, teachers, and children resisted by finding ways to continue their studies. They met in small groups in each other's houses, arriving at different times to avoid suspicion. Meir Sosnowicz, who grew up in the Warsaw Ghetto, remembers:

> *The teacher taught German and Latin. The **Gestapo** arrived in the middle of a lesson and took the teacher away. We heard he was sent to Auschwitz **concentration camp.** We never heard of him again, and the secret lessons stopped.*

Lodz Ghetto Schools

The Nazis seem to have ignored the existence of schools in the Lodz Ghetto. The *Judenrat* ran several schools. The leader of the Council, Chaim Rumkowski, was even able to give out diplomas, as shown in this photo. Perhaps the Nazis allowed it because Rumkowski mostly kept the ghetto running smoothly and carried out Nazi orders. Even where schools were allowed, though, it was hard for children to study. They did not have many supplies and they were also expected to work to make money.

12

Saying No

Some people in the ghettos resisted by refusing to do whatever the Nazis ordered them to do. Each ghetto was run by a *Judenrat*, but the Council was expected to do whatever the Nazis told it to do. If someone refused to join the *Judenrat*, or if a member of the *Judenrat* refused to carry out a Nazi order, he or she was shot. Some people tried cooperating with the Nazis, in the hope of improving things, but soon stopped when they realized there would not be any improvements.

The problem for ghetto resisters was that the Nazis would punish a whole ghetto for the resistance of a single person. The Vilna Ghetto resistance, led by Yitzhak Wittenberg, successfully blew up several German trains. The Nazis were desperate to catch Yitzhak. They told the *Judenrat* of Vilna Ghetto that they would burn down

Keeping a Record

Many people recorded life in the ghettos, despite the fact that if they were caught doing so they would be killed. The Nazis had ordered people to hand in all their cameras, but some people hid theirs and photographed ghetto life. Others wrote about what was going on or painted pictures. The picture above is a painting by Esther Lurie, a young Jewish woman imprisoned in the Kovno Ghetto. Although it looks peaceful, the long line of people on the road are being marched to "the Ninth Fort," a building on the hilltop, to be killed. Esther Lurie survived.

the ghetto unless he gave himself up. The *Judenrat* knew that the Nazis were capable of carrying out their threat, so they persuaded Yitzhak to surrender. He did and the **SS** executed him. The rest of his group fled from the ghetto to the nearby forest to fight as **partisans.**

Revolts

There were revolts—armed uprisings—in many **ghettos,** despite the fact that there was no chance of beating the **Nazis.** The Warsaw Ghetto revolt, in April 1943, is the most famous. However, there were about 40 other revolts in various ghettos.

All of the ghetto revolts were ended by the Nazis, and the **SS** made sure that the punishment was so harsh that the people in the ghetto would not even think of revolting again. From 1942, the Nazis "liquidated" the ghettos one by one, closing them down and **deporting** the people in them to **death camps** and **concentration camps.** People often revolted at the point of deportation, when they felt most desperate and most willing to risk their lives.

The people who organized revolts were mainly young people. Revolts were difficult to organize. First, they had to find enough people willing to take the risk of fighting the Germans. This was not an easy task because most people thought they would live longer if they cooperated and made themselves useful to the Nazis. They saw fighting as certain death, for themselves and others. The next problem was finding enough weapons. Very few people possessed weapons of their own, so they had to find weapons outside the ghetto and smuggle them in. It was hard to do this. Weapons had to be bought on the **black market,** or a local **partisan** group had to be persuaded to give them. A Polish partisan said to one ghetto leader: "Why waste the weapons? You Jews won't fight, or you wouldn't be here."

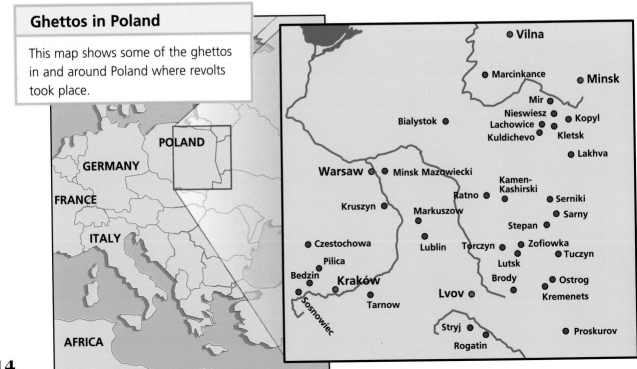

Ghettos in Poland

This map shows some of the ghettos in and around Poland where revolts took place.

Revolt in Kraków

On December 22, 1942, some members of the Kraków Ghetto resistance attacked two cafés that the SS regularly used. Their leader, Dolek Liebeskind, had said of their group: "We are fighting for three lines in the history books." The attack did, however, do some damage—at least twenty SS officers were killed. Many ghetto resistance groups felt as Liebeskind did—that they were not fighting to win but to make sure that their lives, and those of the others in the ghetto, were not forgotten.

The Kraków Ghetto resistance never got enough support for a large scale rising.

The group was right when they said the people of the ghetto would die anyway. The Ghetto was liquidated over March 13 and 14, 1943. The sick, the elderly, and the very young were killed at once. About 2,000 others were sent to Treblinka death camp, like the people in the picture. The rest were sent to Plaszow **labor camp,** which was later liquidated as well.

Czestochowa

The Polish town of Czestochowa, near Kraków, had a ghetto of several thousand people. There was a small resistance group of young people, members of the Jewish Fighting Organization, who were preparing for a revolt.

On January 4, 1943, several of these young people were rounded up by the SS for deportation to Treblinka. Armed with just one knife and a pistol, they decided to fight rather than go. They hoped to start a larger revolt. Mendel Fiszlewicz, their leader, had the pistol and shot at the SS man who was in charge of the round-up.

Fiszlewicz wounded the SS man, but did not kill him. The pistol then jammed, so before he could fire another shot, Fiszlewicz was shot by one of the SS. No other German was harmed.

Even so, the SS took 25 men out of the group waiting to be deported and shot them in front of the others. They then sent the rest off and rounded up an additional 300 women and children and sent them, too. They made it clear that they considered this a "light" punishment, but that even such a "small" show of resistance would be punished.

Resistance in the Camps

Resisting in the **ghettos** was hard. Resisting in the **camps** was even harder. The **Nazis** had set up various camps where, unlike normal prisons, they could imprison anyone without a trial for as long as they wanted. These camps were all run in the same way. Prisoners were worked hard, fed little, and treated appallingly. It was hard for them to live through a normal day, let alone to find the energy to resist.

The **SS** who ran these camps made it as hard as possible for people to make friends or to meet at all. Despite this, many camps had organized resistance groups and, in all camps, people resisted in various ways.

Control in the Camps

The living and working conditions in the camps were so bad that people died every day from starvation, disease, overwork, or the brutality of the SS. Guards watched the prisoners all the time. The SS kept moving people from camp to camp or to different work groups to keep them from forming groups that trusted each other. The SS also had **informers** who listened for plans to rebel or escape. These informers were given "easy" jobs or extra food just for listening—and an even bigger reward for uncovering a plot.

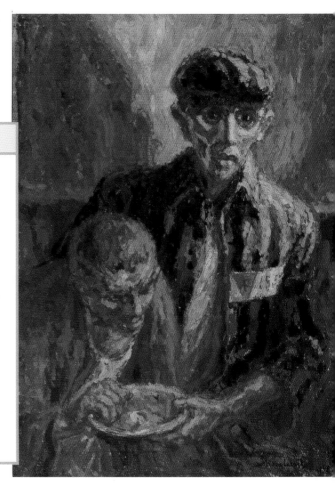

A Different Kind of Resistance

The SS wanted their prisoners, especially their **Jewish** prisoners, to die. Thus, every prisoner who helped another prisoner to survive was resisting the SS. There were many ways to help others. The prisoners could share their food, as the man in the painting is doing. They could try to keep other prisoners hopeful, so they would try harder to stay alive. If they worked in the SS offices, prisoners could get a weak prisoner changed from heavy work to easier work. There are many examples of prisoners who covered up for others who had volunteered for skilled work when they did not really have the skills. If discovered by the SS, they would have been killed.

Muselmen

All camps had people who had given up and were just waiting to die. The prisoners called them *Muselmen,* and feared slipping into this state themselves. Each prisoner had individual ideas about what he or she needed to hang on to in order to keep from becoming *Muselmen.* Prisoners needed something that gave them a feeling of mattering as a person or of being in control, and the SS wanted them to have neither of these things. Roman Frister, who was just twelve when the Nazis sent him to his first camp in 1940, always got up as soon as the **kapo** blew the 5 A.M. whistle. At this point, there were 30 minutes before **roll call.** Frister made himself get up at once and wash. He felt that having, and sticking to, a rule of his own was a way of having a bit of control over his own life.

Recording

Any prisoner who kept a record of what was going on in the camp was risking death. Yet people wrote diaries, drew pictures, and copied SS documents so that what went on in the camps could not be denied. This drawing shows prisoners from a work gang in Auschwitz coming back from work carrying the dead. It was secretly done with a piece of charcoal and scrap cardboard. Once it was drawn, it was carefully hidden away.

Religion

People were not supposed to follow their religion in the camps. Meeting for some kind of religious ceremony, even just a few words of a service, was both a form of resistance and a comfort to prisoners. Catholic priests, Protestant pastors, and Jewish rabbis all held quick services for small groups when they could. People held services without a priest, pastor, or rabbi, too. Hugo Gryn, sent to Auschwitz in 1944, remembers making a secret **menorah** to hold candles for the festival of Hanukkah. He remembers the first night of the Hanukkah festival: "Most of our block gathered around the *menorah*— including some Roman Catholics and several Protestants."

Resistance at Work

Camp prisoners had the chance to resist the **SS** while they were working. They could work slowly, do the work badly, or even make deliberate mistakes. It was dangerous, though. Prisoners were killed if anyone thought they were deliberately doing any of these things. The SS were so intent to stop **sabotage** that they treated many accidents as deliberate.

Hard Labor

Prisoners who were given hard labor, such as clearing roads, working in quarries or mines, and digging ditches, could only really resist if the ***kapo*** in charge of their work gang let them. Some *kapos* let the workers work slowly and replaced tools that broke accidentally without punishment.

Other *kapos* beat slow workers and made workers who broke their tools do their work with their bare hands. Even a sympathetic *kapo* could not let workers get too slow, or they would be in trouble with the SS, who were on the lookout for any sign of resistance. Magda Somogyi, a young **Jewish** woman sent from Hungary to Auschwitz in 1944, remembers working on road repairs in her first camp:

> *Once I dropped a huge stone that was too heavy. The SS man came over and he whipped me for dropping it. Every day, for the next couple of weeks he would whip me before work even started. He said: "You will learn that you do not need to drop the stone."*

These conditions made resistance while working very difficult.

Sabotage

Prisoners like these, photographed in Auschwitz, were only allowed a certain number of mistakes—sometimes none—before a mistake was treated as sabotage.

Sabotage at Dora

Dora camp, in Germany, was set up to make parts for V1 and V2 flying bombs and rockets. Yves Beon, a French Jewish prisoner, remembers:

There were hundreds of ways of making mistakes, if not actually sabotaging things. With different parts of the rocket machinery made in different parts of the factory on different machines, there was often a real problem of fit. So things had to be made to fit and you could do damage there. Also, if you chose carefully you could sabotage something inside, that could not be spotted on final inspection. No one could see rivets badly set or screws hammered (not screwed) in or electrical connects not properly tightened.

A prisoner who had been in Dora painted this picture after the war, showing prisoners hung for sabotage.

War Work

As the war went on, the **Nazis** needed more soldiers to fight, so they took men from the factories and mines, even from the factories that made important war goods. To keep these factories running, the Nazis used camp prisoners.

To make these prisoners grateful and more efficient, the SS gave them rewards—more food, cigarettes, bedding, permission to grow their hair—for working well. Not all prisoners did this kind of work. Jewish prisoners were the least likely to be given this kind of work.

Factory Sabotage

Prisoners who worked in factories had more opportunities for sabotage than those who were digging ditches. Prisoners making uniforms could make them badly so there was a strain across the shoulders or so they did not button right. They could make the seams so loose that they soon split. How much of this they could do varied. Some factories checked work from time to time. Other factories, especially those producing ammunition or weapons, not only had more checks, but also had things marked so that they could be traced back to a particular machine.

Escaping from Nazi Camps

The **Nazis** built their **camps** to keep prisoners in and to punish them by work or by death. One way of resisting was to escape from the camps. At his trial after the war, the Commandant of Auschwitz **concentration camp,** Rudolph Hoess, said:

It was not hard to escape from Auschwitz. The necessary preparations were easily made and it was a simple matter to avoid or outwit the guards.

This was not true. Auschwitz, and all of the other camps, were carefully designed to prevent escapes.

The Camps

Camps were usually some distance from a town or village. Some were walled or, like Mauthausen, created in old forts. Most were surrounded by rings of electrified barbed wire fences, with guardhouses set in them to watch the prisoners. The **SS** often moved people off land close to the camp and discouraged them from using the nearby roads.

Different camps had different levels of security. A small work camp might only have a fence and guard posts. A big camp had more guards, more fences, and more security measures outside the camp. **Death camps,** set up with the one aim of killing large numbers of people, mainly **Jews,** had the tightest security. They were built in remote places and had little contact with the outside world. Because almost everyone was sent straight to death, there were far fewer opportunities for escape, too. Very few people escaped from the death camps.

Auschwitz I and Auschwitz-Birkenau

Auschwitz I was a concentration camp. It had two rows of barbed wire fences around the outside, with guardhouses set all along them (**a**). Auschwitz-Birkenau was a death camp that also kept prisoners alive for a while to work. It had barracks for the prisoners to live in until they were killed. It had more security than Auschwitz I. As well as the same system of outside fencing, Auschwitz-Birkenau was divided into sections, each fenced off, gated, and guarded (**b**).

Prisoners were made to look as different from ordinary people as possible. Their striped uniforms, shaved heads, and, often, starving bodies made them easy to identify. If the camps ran out of uniforms, they gave people ordinary clothes, such as the prisoners shown in the picture here are wearing, but they painted one or more broad stripes down them. The prisoners could not instantly blend in with a crowd. Thus, people who wanted to escape had to get and smuggle out ordinary clothes while in the camp, or they had to have outside help. They had to change the way they looked as soon as possible after escaping.

Planning

Careful planning was vital to an escape. One successful escape from Auschwitz was by four Polish prisoners. Auschwitz was in Poland, so they spoke the local language and could probably hope for help from the local people. They also had help from a **kapo**, who helped them to steal SS uniforms. They worked in the garage of the camp and escaped in an official SS car, with one man still dressed as a prisoner. In this disguise they were unlikely to be stopped and questioned by Nazi soldiers. Escapes that needed planning and help were more likely to work, but they were also more likely to be discovered by the SS.

Hans Bonarewitz escaped from Mauthausen camp by hiding in a wooden packing case on a truck driving out of the camp. He was caught eighteen days after he escaped and executed.

Timing

Because the camps were carefully guarded, many prisoners tried to escape while out of the camp, as part of a work gang. Usually one prisoner, or at the most two, were involved in these escapes—it was easier for a single person to get away unnoticed. Camp breakouts needed more people working together to be successful.

Camp Revolts

The hardest kind of resistance to organize in the **camps,** and so the rarest, was revolt. Revolts needed as many people and weapons as possible. Even with these, the chances of success were so low as to seem suicidal. There were many more prisoners than guards, but the guards were fit and had a huge supply of weapons and equipment. Revolts also needed careful planning. It was hard for resisters to meet and plan in the camps and hard to find enough trustworthy people. It is impossible to know how many camp revolts failed at the planning stage because **informers** told the **SS** about them—probably a lot.

No Other Chance

The revolts we know most about happened in the **death camps.** People taken to death camps did revolt. They had little chance for any other kind of resistance. They also had very little to lose. What kept people in the other camps from revolting was the hope that they would somehow live through the horror, whereas if they revolted they were almost certain to be killed. People taken to the death camps were going to die anyway. For this reason, revolts in other types of camps often took place towards the end of the war, when it became clear to the prisoners that the **Nazis** were losing and that the camps would be shut and all of the prisoners shot.

Death March Revolts

Once the **Allies** began to advance into Nazi-held land, the Nazis moved people to camps closer to, and then inside, Germany. Sometimes prisoners were transported in trucks or by train. Most often, they had to march. These marches took place in the early months of 1945, in the middle of a bad winter. The marches were called death marches because so many people died on them. The weather and illness killed many. Others were shot by the SS. There were revolts by prisoners on these marches, too. Prisoners also escaped, though few survived the weather. This photo was taken after the war. It shows prisoners shot while on a death march and piled into a pit.

Destruction at Auschwitz-Birkenau

In early October 1944, there was a revolt among the *Sonderkommando* (SK) at Auschwitz-Birkenau. The SK units were Jewish men who had to clear out the **gas chambers** and burn the corpses. There were four crematoria for burning bodies at Auschwitz, and hundreds of SK personnel. Some Jewish girls working in a nearby factory smuggled out some explosives and passed them on to members of the SK. The revolt broke out on October 7, 1944. The SS acted quickly, but several prisoners managed to escape, although they were all later caught. Crematorium IV was set on fire and Crematorium II was so badly damaged that the SS had to finish the job and blow it up. The remains of Crematorium II are pictured here. Most of the men who took part in the revolt were killed either during the revolt or executed after it. The women who had smuggled out the explosives were executed, too.

Revolt at Treblinka

One of the earliest revolts was at Treblinka death camp, on August 2, 1943. Most people who arrived at Treblinka were herded straight to their deaths, but there were a few hundred *Arbeitsjuden*—"Work Jews"—kept alive to run the camp. These people were regularly killed and replaced with new arrivals. Some of the *Arbeitsjuden* had made a copy of the key to the weapons store and had stolen some weapons and gasoline. On the afternoon of August 2 the camp was "disinfected" as usual, but the sprayers were filled with gasoline, not disinfectant. The resisters then set fire to the buildings. Several SS and many **kapos** were shot in the battle that followed. About 150 people escaped. Of these, a hundred were hunted down. Treblinka was never rebuilt. The area where the camp was was turned into a farm.

Individuals Who Helped

Oscar Schindler

Oscar Schindler was a German **Nazi** who took the chance offered by the Nazi invasion of Poland to take over a factory making kitchen equipment in Kraków. The factory used **Jewish** workers from the **ghetto.** Schindler did not speak out against the Nazis' treatment of the Jews. He was helpful and friendly and even socialized with the **SS** men who ran the **camps.** The first Jews that Schindler helped, he helped for profit. He suggested to rich Jews that if they "invested" in his factory, they could work there.

A Change of Heart?

In the summer of 1942, Schindler saw a round-up of people in the ghetto. They were herded into trucks for **deportation.** He later wrote: "After this, no thinking person could fail to see what would happen. I decided to do everything in my power to defeat their system."

History As a Story

In 1993, director Steven Spielberg made a movie about Oscar Schindler and the Jewish people he helped. It was based on the book *Schindler's List* by Thomas Keneally. Neither the book nor the film were straight factual histories of the time, but both took care to get the factual details right. The film won several different awards, and millions of people went to see it. Many of them were made aware of the horrors of the **Holocaust** for the first time by this film.

Schindler began by asking for more Jewish workers for his factory. He made sure that they were treated and fed well. He asked the commandant of the Plaszow camp, Amon Goeth, if a sub-camp could be set up by his factory for about 1,000 workers "to save time otherwise wasted traveling to work." Goeth agreed. This sub-camp had SS guards, like all camps. Schindler had to walk a careful line between helping the Jews and not being suspected. He bribed the guards not to talk about the fact that the prisoners got about twice as much food a day as in Plaszow, better barracks, medical care, and reasonable working conditions. Not all guards stayed bought. Schindler was arrested twice for helping the Jews. Both times he talked his way out of it.

Going Further

In 1944, the Nazis pulled out of Kraków. Schindler got permission to move his factory to Brünnlitz, Czechoslovakia, and to take his workers with him. There was a mix-up at the station and 300 of his workers were taken to Auschwitz instead. Schindler did not let go of them. Anna Duklauer Perl, one of those workers, remembers:

> We just had to hope that Schindler would come for us. We were there for a few weeks and were just being taken for a shower (and wondering if it would be water or gas) when he arrived. He said: "What are you doing with these people, these are my people!"

They were the only group of Jews to be taken out of Auschwitz at the time.

After the War

Between 1943 and 1945, Schindler saved over 1,500 Jews. When the war ended, Schindler made a speech to the workers he had protected for so long:

> My children, you are saved. Germany has lost the war. Prove yourselves worthy of the millions of victims and behave humanely and with justice. Leave the judging and avenging to those who are responsible for it.

Schindler himself did not have a lucky life after the war. He was not wanted in Germany, and the U.S. refused to give him a visa because he had been a member of the Nazi Party. Schindler and his wife went to Argentina, where they tried to set up a farm with some of the people he had saved. The farm did not do well.

In 1958 Schindler went back to Germany and tried, but failed, to start another business. He found that many Germans still disapproved of what he had done and were unwilling to work with him. He ended up relying on the people he had saved. They looked after him well, sending him money when he needed it and paying for him to travel to Israel for regular reunions. Schindler died in 1974 and was buried in Jerusalem.

Irene Gut Opdyke

Irene Gut Opdyke was a seventeen-year-old Polish girl studying to be a nurse in Radom, Poland, when the German and **Soviet** armies invaded Poland. As a young Polish girl she was in a very different position from Oscar Schindler, the German **Nazi** businessman. Yet she still found a way to resist the Nazis.

Irene and some of the patients and staff at the hospital fled Radom when the invasion began, but they were captured by the Russians. Irene eventually got back to Radom in 1940 and found her family. She was caught in a Nazi round-up of Poles to work in their factories. She worked in an ammunition factory, but the work was hard. One day she fainted during an inspection. Often those too sick to work were **deported,** but because Irene spoke good German she was sent to work in the Nazi officers' mess—where they ate and relaxed. She organized the Polish workers for the German man in charge of the mess, Herr Schultz, who was kind to her and gave her food for her family.

Helping People

Irene, more settled herself, became aware of the situation of **Jewish** people, and began to help:

*From one room you could see the Glinice **Ghetto.** One day I heard shooting. Men, women, and children were running through the ghetto streets. **SS** men were spilling out of trucks and shooting at the fleeing Jews. Through the glass I heard screaming and the barking of dogs. The snow darkened with blood. I had just seen the Germans' answer to their "Jewish Problem." The next afternoon I slipped outside and made a hole in the fence that backed onto the ghetto. From the pail of potato peelings I took out a tin box I had filled with cheese and apples. I wedged it into the hole and hurried back to the kitchen. The next day the box was empty. I collected it and went back to work for the Nazis. Every day now I found a chance to slip food under the fence.*

A Clearer View

Irene Gut Opdyke could only see into the Glinice Ghetto from above the high walls that surrounded it. In other ghettos it was far easier to see the appalling conditions people were living in. This photo shows part of the Warsaw Ghetto separated from the rest of Warsaw by barbed wire fencing.

More Help

The German army moved on, to Lvov and then Ternopol. Irene went too, and was given more and more responsibility. In Ternopol she ran the laundry:

> *The laundry used Jewish workers from the local work camp. There were twelve of them. "I'll bring you food when I can," I said. "I'll look after you." Moses Steiner, a stooped and gloomy man, made a small shrug. "You're only a young girl," he said. "What can you do?"*

Irene did look after them, bringing them food and passing on things she heard while waiting on the Nazi officers. Then they asked for more help:

> *One day Herschl Morris said: "My brother and I want to join the **partisans** in the forest. Irene, you must help us to get there." I did not become a resistance fighter, a smuggler of Jews, a defier of the Nazis all at once. First steps are always small: I began by hiding food under a fence. Now I was smuggling Jews to the Janowka forest.*

Irene smuggled more people, and food for them, to the forest regularly. Then she became housekeeper to a major and hid the remaining laundry workers in his villa. As the Russian army closed in, Irene had to move on with the army again, to Kielce.

With the Partisans

In Kielce, Irene ran away and joined a group of partisans.

> *They gave me small jobs to begin with, to test my nerve and loyalty. I tucked messages into the thick bun of my hair and carried them between the partisans and their spies who worked for the Germans. Sometimes I carried packages of money, smuggled in from England, to buy guns or to pass on to a group further up the line. I was never told more than I needed to know.*

At the end of the war, Irene tried to find her family. She was arrested as a partisan but escaped. After spending some time in a **displaced persons camp,** she emigrated to the United States.

The Franks

The Frank family is famous, thanks to the diary kept by a young girl named Anne Frank. Many people, if asked to name a **Jewish** child caught up in the **Holocaust**, would name Anne Frank. Far fewer people know the names of the Dutch people who helped her family and their friends, the van Pels, to hide. Yet without the help of these people it would have been impossible for them all to hide for long.

Who Helped the Franks?

The people who helped the Franks were all people who worked in the offices of Otto Frank's business. The Franks had left Germany for Amsterdam, in the Netherlands, to escape the **Nazis** in 1933. When the Nazis invaded the Netherlands, Anne's father, Otto, planned a secret hiding place for the family in the offices where he worked. Some of the office workers had to know what was going on and had to be prepared to help for the plan to work.

These people were Miep Gies, Jo Kleiman, Victor Kugler, and Bep Voskuijl. Miep's husband, Jan, had already been trusted with taking over part of the Frank business when Jews were banned from owning businesses. Jo Kleiman took over the rest. However, "looking after" business was one thing; actively helping and hiding Jews was far more dangerous. Their families knew what the helpers were doing and sometimes helped, too. Bep's father built the bookcase that hid the stairs to the secret annex, and her sister made clothes for Anne and Margot, Anne's sister, as they grew out of their old ones.

Hidden Away

This photo shows the bookcase that hid the stairs of the secret annex in the Frank's factory. When the door was shut, the bookcase was flat against the wall, underneath the map.

Keeping Things Going

Victor Kugler and Jo Kleiman had a big responsibility. Jo and his brother helped to get the secret annex ready. Meanwhile, Jo and Victor ran the business. They had to deal with any questions the Nazis had—and even the questions that traveling salesmen or workers in the warehouse asked about noises or lights. Anne wrote in her diary: "Kugler, who at times finds the enormous responsibility for the eight of us overwhelming, can hardly talk from the built-up tension and strain."

Food

Bep and Miep were responsible for feeding the people in hiding. At the time, food was **rationed,** but somehow the helpers found enough food to feed eight extra people. Before the families went into hiding, Herman van Pels—who had worked in the meat and sausage business—took Miep to meet a local butcher who was prepared to give her meat without ration cards. If the Nazis had caught the butcher, they would have hanged him.

Found Out

When the Franks and their friends were betrayed, their helpers were also in trouble. Victor and Jo were arrested along with those in hiding on August 4, 1944. Victor remembers:

*There were four police officers, one in **Gestapo** uniform. He made me show him round the building. The three Dutch policemen made for the bookcase. The moment that I had feared for years had come.*

Victor and Jo were sent to prison, interrogated, and listed as "asocials." They were sent to Amersfoort Police **Transit Camp** on September 11, 1944. Jo was released on September 18 with a burst ulcer. Victor was sent to a **labor camp.** He escaped at the beginning of March 1945 and stayed free until the Netherlands was **liberated.** The arresting officers did not think that Miep and Bep were involved, so they were not arrested. They kept the business running. They also saved Anne's diary.

Occasional Help

Some people were not part of an escape line, but helped from time to time, or even only once. In 1943 Christabel Bielenburg, a British woman married to a German, was living in Berlin. She hid a **Jewish** couple for two nights because a friend was desperate for somewhere to put them. Other friends of hers in the French Resistance told her not to because, as a foreigner, she was watched by the **Nazi** blockwarden and she had young children who might talk. She took them in anyway: "They left after two days, in the night. They left me a note of thanks, for two miserable days of grace. I never knew what happened to them."

Escape Lines

There were many people, all over **occupied** Germany, who risked their lives as part of a chain of helpers getting as many Jews out as possible. The **Gestapo** and the **SS** were constantly trying to find and break up these escape lines. Those who were caught knew they would be shot or hung for helping Jews to escape— probably only after they had been tortured first to give up the names of other people in the group. So these groups told everyone involved as little as possible.

A Berlin Escape Line

Bernt Engelmann, a German who is now an author and journalist, became part of an escape line:

> *Annie Ney ran a café and made it clear she had no love for the Nazis, but after all, she was just an old lady who had trouble getting around and treated everyone kindly. She was talking to me one day about a Jewish girl who needed to escape. An SS man came in to buy cakes and pastries. She stayed calm. "It looks as if someone's having a birthday party," she remarked. "Yours, Herr Sturmbannfuhrer? Congratulations." She gave him a free glass of brandy and chatted until he left.*

Just Once

Christabel Bielenburg only hid Jews once. Her anti-Nazi German friends were angry that she did it because she was already under suspicion as an Englishwoman and had two young children who could give her away at any time.

Good Contacts?

People who owned hotels, cafés, and restaurants were in a good position to be part of an escape line. People came and went in these places, so it was easy to pass on messages, to meet over a cup of coffee, or to spend time waiting to be picked up. Of course, the Gestapo and the SS were well aware of this and kept an eye on these places. Café owners had to walk a thin line between being friendly to the Gestapo and SS who were in and out, and being too friendly—making them

suspicious. These Nazi officers are sitting at tables outside a café in Paris during the Nazi **occupation** of France.

One Escape

Annie Ney's contacts included a schoolteacher, Fräulein Bonse, and a tailor who made suits for the SS, Herr Desch. Her husband's bakery van made regular deliveries over the border: sometimes it carried escapees. This group helped Grete Nussbaum to escape. Grete was a young Jewish woman who, because she was blonde, had been pretending not to be Jewish. However, she needed **papers** and was nearly caught. Fräulein Bonse heard the Gestapo were looking for Grete and told her to go to Annie Ney's café:

The café owner came over and shook hands. "Everything is taken care of," she said. "Our delivery man will pick you up at about 3 P.M. and take you to the house of good friends. You can stay there for a few days—by Saturday you'll be somewhere safe."

Everything went as planned. Grete was taken to a large country house near the Dutch border. There, a German family acted as if she was an expected visitor. They booked her into a room in a hotel just across the border. The next day a priest came and gave her a ticket to London, some money, a baggage receipt for luggage already in London, and an invitation from the British Academic Exchange Service for a six-month stay.

Resistance Groups

There was organized resistance all through Germany and the lands it took over during the war. The groups who resisted fell into two main types. **Partisans** were secret armies. They lived in hiding and fought the **Nazis** with weapons wherever possible. Resistance workers were ordinary people who carried on with their everyday lives under Nazi occupation. Many of them even worked for the Nazis, or were friendly with them, hoping to pick up useful information.

Partisans

Partisans included resisters who had escaped from **camps** or **ghettos,** or were being hunted by the Nazis for political activities. Most partisan groups belonged to a single ethnic or national group—for example, there were Polish partisans, Russian partisans, and **Jewish** partisans.

Working Together?

Not all partisan groups were happy to work with others, even if they both saw the Nazis as their enemies. Many partisans hid in forests, often competing with other groups for food, space, and shelter. Jewish escapees were particularly at risk. Many partisan groups in German-**occupied** Russia and Poland were **anti-Semitic.**

The Bielski Partisans

This photo shows some Bielski partisans who lived in the woods near Novogrodek, in Nazi-occupied Russia. Led by the Bielski brothers, the group helped people escape from the Novogrodek Ghetto. It also attacked Nazi headquarters in nearby towns and Nazi troops on the move. Dov Cohen, who escaped from the Novogrodek Ghetto to join the Bielskis, remembers his feelings at his first sight of the partisans:

We could hardly believe our eyes: armed Jewish men who I knew well from Novogrodek, who had escaped from the ghetto. They were no longer pale, frightened, and downtrodden. They stood tall and proud. And, most

important of all: they were armed with pistols, rifles, submachine guns, and even machine guns.

This photo shows a German supply train that was derailed by a Polish partisan group. Railway lines were a favorite target for partisans. Stopping the trains kept the Nazis from moving soldiers and war supplies. It also stopped **transports** to the camps.

What Did the Partisans Do?

All partisans tried to disrupt Nazi rule. How they did this depended on exactly where they were, how large their group was, and how well armed they were. Irene Gut Opdyke remembers: "We worked with other groups sometimes, but mostly our attacks were made when we saw a chance to act."

Blowing up or burning down Nazi headquarters or damaging roads, bridges, and railway lines all disrupted Nazi government. Ambushing a truck full of German weapons not only stopped the Nazis from using the weapons, but it also armed the partisans. If a group was large enough and well armed, they even attacked the German army on the march. However, even groups that did not have guns and ammunition could still be effective.

Did the Partisans Succeed?

The partisans could not beat the entire German army, but they did disrupt Nazi rule. The Nazis were furious that they could not catch the partisans and that there were so many—about 20,000 just in the Nalibocka forest in Poland. So many thousands of people working against the Nazis, even on a small scale, caused a lot of damage. On just one mission, a group of partisans from the Rudnicka forest in Poland blew up a train carrying ammunition. They destroyed the guns and ammunition aboard, and killed 50 soldiers. Partisans also gave people hope, showing that the Nazis could be resisted.

Resistance Movements

There were resistance movements all across **Nazi-occupied** Europe, even in Germany itself. **Partisans** were hard to catch because they lived in hiding, often in forests that they knew well and the German soldiers sent in after them did not know at all. Resistance workers were hard to catch because they carried on with their ordinary lives, even pretending to help the Nazis.

What Did Resistance Movements Do?

Various resistance groups organized escape routes for **Allied** troops trapped in Nazi territory, as well as for escapees from various Nazi **camps.** They blew up roads, railways, bridges, and telephone lines to disrupt Nazi communications.

Who Joined Resistance Movements?

Many different people joined the resistance, for many different reasons. Men and women, young and old, worked together against the Nazis. Most resistance groups and escape lines were organized so that each person knew only a few people in the group. If the Nazis caught a resistance member and forced them to name the others, they were only able to name a few people.

For this reason, the Nazis were always trying to get a Nazi supporter into the resistance, either as a resistance worker

The July Plot

The Nazis tried to stamp out any resistance inside Germany as soon as they came to power in 1933. Even so, there were always people working against the Nazis, dangerous though it was. There were several attempts to assassinate Hitler, on the assumption that if Hitler was dead, Nazi policies would collapse. Toward the end of World War II, even German army officers were resisting Nazi policies. Lieutenant General von Witzleben, pictured here, fought for Germany and was a respected German officer. Even so, he took part in a plot to assassinate Hitler in July 1944 by planting a bomb in Hitler's headquarters. The bomb went off, but Hitler had changed the meeting place planned for the basement to another room. The plotters who were caught were all hung by piano wire strung from meat hooks.

or as an escapee. If this supporter could fool an escape line into believing he was a British airman who had been shot down, he could travel along a whole escape line, thus finding out who all of the members were.

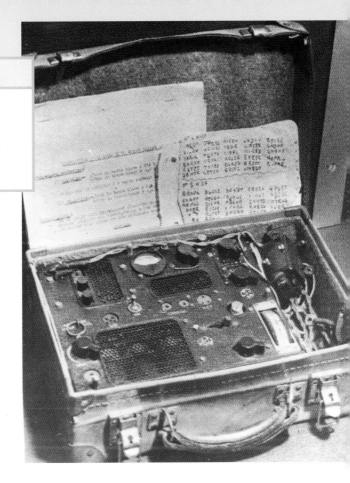

Len Arlington

Len Arlington was a British soldier, sent to fight in France in 1939. He was captured by the invading German army in the summer of 1940. Len escaped and made his way back to Gondecourt, France, to hide with French friends. The local resistance asked Len to help them question people who said they were escapees, British airmen, in need of help. They were—Len even knew one of them. He took them down the escape line and ran into trouble at a particular house:

> *Madame Sangrez said she was waiting for a signal. I waited with her. A plane, a German plane, flew over and she said: "That's the signal; the British will be coming for you tomorrow night." My danger-sensing nerve began to twitch and I told the others we should get out, quick. We left next day, saying we were heading for the coast, but actually going back to Gondecourt.*

They got back, only for the two airmen to go to a local bar, get very drunk, and begin singing in front of a group of Nazis. Luckily the Nazis were drunk, too, and Len managed to get the men out. The next day the two airmen set off to try to escape on their own. Len never found out if they made it.

Outside Help

Resistance movements all over the countries occupied by the Nazis had help from the Allies who were fighting Germany. The British formed a Special Operations Executive **(SOE)** to send people, weapons, other supplies, and money to occupied countries, to the resistance, and to the partisans. Polish partisan Irene Gut Opdyke remembers that one of her jobs was to deliver packages of money from Britain to people who needed it:

> *An officer stopped me as I wheeled my bicycle across a guarded bridge. I flirted with him, using my best German, promising to return after visiting my mother. Meanwhile a wrapped parcel [package] of thousands of British pounds lay in the basket between the handlebars.*

Church Help

Did the various churches in Germany and **Nazi-occupied** lands do anything to resist the Nazis? Most of the resistance to the **Holocaust** came from individual people with strong religious beliefs, not from any church as a whole.

The German Churches

When the Nazis came to power in 1933, Hitler, the Nazi leader, saw religion as competition for the loyalty of the German people. However, he needed church support until he was safely in power. So, he stressed the ideas that he and the churches shared, such as belief in the family. German churches did not openly oppose the Nazis at first. However, they did oppose the Nazi **euthanasia** program, set up in 1933.

The Nazis persuaded the relatives of mentally and physically disabled Germans to put them into clinics, promising that the state would care for them. Instead, they killed them. Catholic bishops and Protestant pastors led protests against this killing. The Nazis worried that the German people would react badly to the news. They pretended to abandon the project, but continued it in secret. About 50,000 disabled people were murdered. As the Nazi grip on Germany tightened, it became clear to church leaders that the Nazis would not tolerate any opposition. They feared that encouraging people to resist would be encouraging them to make themselves targets for Nazi persecution.

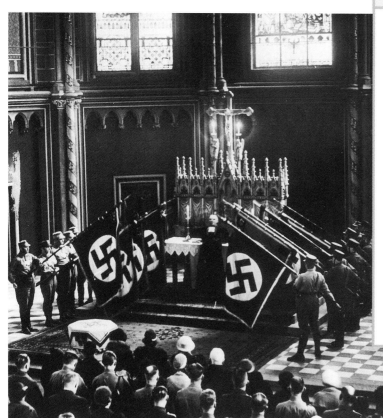

Working With the Nazis?

This photo was taken in a Protestant church in 1934. The Nazi banners are almost hiding the altar.

When the Nazis first came to power, their ideas about family, good behavior, and the government caring for the poor were seen as good things by both the Catholic and Protestant churches. They ignored Nazi **anti-Semitism.** Hitler hid the fact that he wanted to control religion, just like every other part of life. It did not take long, however, for it to become clear.

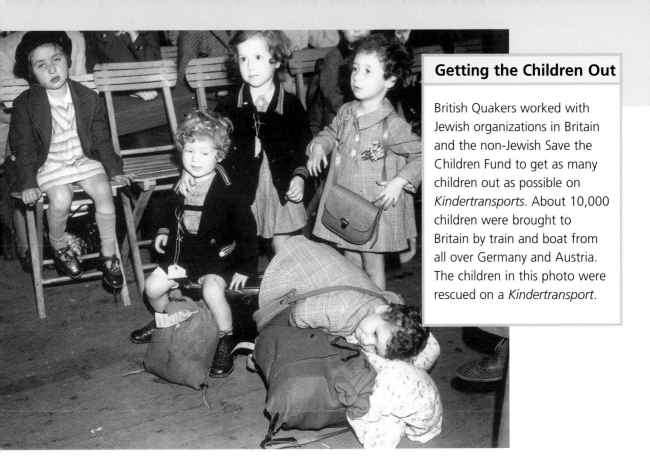

Getting the Children Out

British Quakers worked with Jewish organizations in Britain and the non-Jewish Save the Children Fund to get as many children out as possible on *Kindertransports*. About 10,000 children were brought to Britain by train and boat from all over Germany and Austria. The children in this photo were rescued on a *Kindertransport*.

Churches Outside Germany

Churches in countries occupied by the Nazis faced the same problems as the churches inside Germany. Open criticism gave the Nazis the excuse they needed to persecute the churches. Again, there was resistance by church members, but only on an individual level. In some cases, whole groups of believers did resist. For example, church orphanages hid **Jewish** children.

It was easier for churches in countries outside German control to resist the Nazis. British **Quakers** worked hard to get **refugees** out of Germany in the early 1930s. Victor Klemperer, a German Jew who was married to an **Aryan** German, had been trying to get out of Germany with increasing desperation since 1935.

In 1938, Klemperer wrote in his diary: "I had written to Lima, to Jerusalem, to Sydney, and to the Quakers via Miss Livingstone."

Miss Livingstone was an English Quaker, living in Berlin, who was using her links to the Quaker church in England to try to get non-Aryans out of Germany. Klemperer was put in touch with her too late for her to help. He and his wife had to leave their home and move to one of the "Jewish houses" for Jewish/Aryan couples. In 1945, just as he was told he was to be **deported,** the **Allies** bombed Dresden. Klemperer pulled off the yellow star the Germans made him and other Jews wear, and in the confusion he and his wife escaped and hid until the end of the war.

Individual Resistance

Many people had religious beliefs that caused them to oppose the **Nazis.** Some of them worked in escape networks. Those who lived in Nazi-**occupied** lands worked secretly, while seeming to accept—even to work with—the Nazis.

Encouraging Others to Help

Catholic priests and Protestant pastors were important in their communities. Their attitude toward the Nazis could influence the people who went to their churches. In 1938, *Kristallnacht*, a Nazi-led time of rioting and destruction of **Jewish** synagogues, businesses, and homes, shocked many priests and pastors.

Pastor von Jan said in a sermon to his German congregation: "Much evil has been done, both secretly and openly." Shortly after saying this, he was arrested and sent to a **concentration camp.**

Individual clergy in occupied Europe also resisted the Nazis. A French pastor named Andre Trocme encouraged his congregation to help smuggle Jewish people out of France to safety in Switzerland. Perhaps these people would have helped anyway, but Trocme got them working together and feeling confident enough to help. The villagers saved over 4,000 Jews between 1940 and the end of the war in 1945.

Taking in the Children

Some Christians took in Jewish children to keep them safe. If possible, they were passed off as family members. If they looked too different to be described as "cousins" or too much like the Nazi stereotype of Jews, they were kept in hiding. Various religious organizations helped, too. Orphanages run by Catholics and Protestants also took in Jewish children and hid them; they had organizations that gave these children different identities. The boy to the left of the priest (front row) is Shloymele Gziewacz. He spent the war pretending to be a Catholic named Marek Kaczinski.

Help for the Partisans

Many Catholic priests or Protestant pastors helped **partisan** groups or the resistance in occupied countries. Some joined the partisans in hiding, while others helped by passing messages and supplies. Irene Gut Opdyke remembered that the local Catholic priest performed a special ceremony for joining the partisans.

Help in the Camps

There were Catholic priests, Protestant pastors, and Jewish rabbis imprisoned in concentration camps. They all helped people in the **camps** by holding secret services and trying to keep people hopeful. Some of them also helped in more immediate ways. On February 17, 1941, Father Maximilian Kolbe was one of the Polish monks arrested and imprisoned when a monastery was broken up. On May 28, 1941, he was sent to Auschwitz camp. On July 29, the camp commander announced that ten prisoners were to be starved to death as a punishment for the escape of a prisoner. Kolbe stepped forward and offered himself in the place of one of the prisoners. The **SS** let him trade places. At the end of two weeks, Kolbe was the only one of the ten still alive. He was killed by an injection to the heart. The prisoner he saved survived the war.

While some clergy spoke out against the Nazis, others tried to help people in the camps by seeming to accept the Nazis and asking them for favors for prisoners in the camps. Sometimes this worked. In December 1940, the Archbishop of Kraków asked if prisoners in Auschwitz camp could have Christmas packages and was given permission. Nazi favors only went so far, however. He was not allowed to hold a Christmas mass in the camp.

Countries that Helped

The governments of some countries resisted the **Nazi Holocaust.** If a country was **occupied** by the Nazis, then it found it hard to resist Nazi demands. What a government decided to do often depended on how tight Nazi control of their country was. The government of occupied France cooperated with the Nazis in their persecution of the **Jews,** even as they resisted the occupation of their country. The French sent 77,000 Jewish men, women, and children to their deaths. Other occupied countries actively worked to save the Jews living there— only eight Finnish Jews were **deported.**

Italy

Italy, ruled by Mussolini, fought on the side of Germany until 1943. Hitler and Mussolini (left), shown here meeting in Berlin in 1938, both believed in themselves as the single ruler of their nation. They both believed in controlling the country completely, using the army and police. So at first, they were happy to work together against other countries that believed in different sorts of government. While the Italians controlled their own government, no Jews were deported from Italy to the **death camps** in German-occupied Poland. The Nazis urged the Italians to hand over the Jews from countries they occupied, if not from Italy itself. Mussolini's commanders refused. In 1943, the Italian government surrendered to the **Allies.** Before the Allies could physically occupy Italy, the German army occupied the country and **SS** units began to round up Jews.

Bulgaria

Bulgaria had cooperated with the Nazis in return for being allowed to run its own affairs under Nazi control, rather than being occupied completely. In March 1943, the Nazis ordered the Bulgarians to deport the 12,000 Jews in the parts of Greece and Yugoslavia they had taken over. They did so. The Nazis then told them to deport all Bulgarian Jews.

The king of Bulgaria, its parliament, its church, and many of its people refused. The king overturned all of the anti-Jewish laws that had been set up under Nazi control and freed all of the Jews that were in **camps** in Bulgaria. Farmers in the north threatened to lie down on the railway lines, to stop trains from taking Jews out of the country. The Nazis realized that it would take too much time and too many German soldiers to overcome this level of resistance. No Bulgarian Jews were deported.

Pope Pius XII

The attitude of the Catholic Pope Pius XII, in white in the photo, shows how complicated dealing with the Nazi persecution of the Jews could become. The Pope lived in Vatican City, an independent part of Italy, in Rome. Pius XII had been forced to cooperate with the Nazis when they came to power in Germany in order to limit Nazi-encouraged anti-Catholic violence. He did not speak out openly against Nazi persecution of the Jews or urge Catholics in occupied lands to help Jewish people. This would have been telling them to put themselves in danger. However, in 1939 he told his bishops, in a non-public announcement, to help Jewish people when they could.

When the Nazis invaded Italy in 1943, the Pope told the Vatican City and the Catholic churches, convents, and monasteries of Rome to shelter as many Jews as possible. He persuaded the German officer in charge of deportations in Rome to stop deporting Jewish people.

Denmark

The German army marched into Denmark in April 1940. The Danes resisted the Nazi takeover. King Christian X and the Danish churches asked the Danish people to help any Jews they could. They even closed Danish universities so the students could help Jews to escape. Notices went up saying: "Stand in front of your Jewish neighbors' homes and don't let them be taken away! Hide their children! Move into the **ghettos** with them!"

The Nazis planned a big round-up of Jewish people on the night of October 1, 1943. The Danes heard about it and rushed to get people out. Over 7,000 people were smuggled to Sweden by boat. Others were hidden. The SS only found 500 Jews, mostly old or sick people who could not escape. They were sent to Terezín Ghetto. The Danish government insisted that the SS look after them, and checked regularly. Because of this, despite the fact that so many were old when they were taken to the ghetto, 423 survived the war.

Finland

Soldiers from the **Soviet Union** invaded Finland on November 30, 1939. At this time, the Soviet Union was an ally of Germany, so the Finnish government cooperated with the **Nazis.** The Finnish police even began to **deport Jewish** people in February 1943. However, news reached Finland that only one of the eight Jews deported reached Auschwitz alive. The Finnish opposition party and many important Finnish clergy protested to the government. Ordinary Finns protested, too. So, the government refused to deport any more Jews.

Hungary

At first, the Hungarian government worked with the Nazis, rather than be taken over by them. They refused to give up their Jews, though. In March 1944, the German army marched into Hungary. The Nazis took over, and the deportation of Hungarian Jews straight to the **gas chambers** of Auschwitz-Birkenau began. The Hungarian government did not try to stop the deportations until the U.S. threatened to bomb Budapest. At that point, the government refused to deport any more Jews. It was too late for these Hungarian Jews, photographed by the **SS** just before they were forced into the gas chambers at Auschwitz-Birkenau.

Turkey

The Turkish government took in German **refugees** before war broke out. It did not take sides in the war. However, it did help Jewish people to escape the Nazis, despite the fact that, as the Nazis advanced, Turkey was under a lot of pressure from Germany to become an ally or be taken over. Turkish embassies in France protected their Jewish people from Nazi laws, rescued them from **camps,** and even took them off trains bound for the **death camps.** They sent these people to Turkey, through Nazi-**occupied** land. The Turkish government was not always helpful to non-Turkish Jews. It turned away boatloads of refugees with no visas. However, the government also told all of their embassies to "provide all possible assistance" to persecuted Jews and many Jewish escape groups were allowed to operate from Turkey.

Ignoring the Rules

Sometimes a country helped Jews who were trying to escape without meaning to. Embassy workers sometimes ignored the rules set up by their countries in order to give out visas and **papers** that refugees needed. Some of these workers suffered for their actions. They lost their jobs, or were imprisoned. People who worked for private agencies, not governments, also worked hard to get documents for Jews. Varian Fry, who worked for the American Emergency Rescue Committee in Marseilles, France, set up a team to provide papers, mostly forged, to get 1,500 people (who had been refused visas by the American embassy) out of France.

Aristides de Sousa Mendes

Aristides de Sousa Mendes worked in the Portuguese embassy at Bordeaux, in France. Jews who wanted to go to the U.S. or Canada had to do so from Lisbon and needed a transit visa to cross Spain and Portugal. The Spanish would not let refugees in without a Portuguese transit visa. The Portuguese government told Sousa Mendes not to give out any visas.

As the Germans got closer and closer to the Spanish border, Sousa Mendes drove to the border town of Hendaye. He walked through the streets and gave out 10,000 visas. On June 23, 1940, the Portuguese ambassador in Spain arrived and told the border guards not to accept any more of Sousa Mendes' visas. He also told Sousa Mendes that he had to go back to Portugal. On his return to Portugal, Mendes was fired. He could not find any other work because of what he had done.

Others Who Helped

Many embassy people helped refugees. Frank Foley, from the British embassy in Berlin, helped many Jews to escape to Palestine. A Japanese diplomat, Chiune Sugihara, in Kovno, Lithuania, gave out 3,400 visas that allowed refugees to cross the Soviet Union and China to go to Shanghai. A Swedish diplomat, Raoul Wallenberg, saved tens of thousands of Jews in Hungary. He gave out visas and set up safe houses that he claimed as "Swedish territory" meaning the Nazis could not arrest the Jews inside them. This photo shows a Swedish letter of protection for Lili Katz, one of the Hungarian Jews Wallenberg helped.

The Warsaw Ghetto Revolt

In 1939, the **Nazis** began to set up **ghettos** in big cities and to move **Jewish** people from the city and the surrounding countryside into them. Warsaw was one of these cities, and the ghetto, walled off in October 1939, was the biggest of all. Wladyslaw Szpilman, who survived the ghetto, remembers that, even after increasingly harsh laws against Jews, the sealing off came as a surprise:

> *In the second half of November, without any explanation, the Germans began barricading the north end of Marszalkowska street with barbed wire. We were told we had to wear white armbands with a blue star of David when we were out of the house. Then the Jewish* **deportees** *from the west began to arrive. The gates of the ghetto were closed on November 15.*

Almost half a million people were crammed into just 1.3 square miles (3.4 square kilometers). There were, on average, seven people in each room. In fact, the ghetto developed its own social levels. People who were important in the ghetto might have a room to themselves, while in the most run-down areas there were many more people living in one room.

The *Judenrat*

The *Judenrat*, the Jewish Council that ran the ghetto, was led by Adam Czerniakow. He was sure that as long as the Jews worked for the Nazis, they would be kept alive because they were useful. So, he and the Council cooperated with the Nazis. They provided workers for local businesses and factories and even managers to run them. He made speeches assuring people that cooperating with the Nazis was better for them. If they resisted, they would be shot. If they cooperated, they would live. Things were not that simple, as Czerniakow soon found out.

Food Coupons

The *Judenrat* organized everything, including the inadequate food supplies. The people in this photo are in line for official food coupons.

A High Death Rate

Starvation and disease killed hundreds a day in the Warsaw Ghetto. There was no time or space for proper burials. Bodies were piled into carts and taken to mass graves, as shown in this picture. One survivor of the ghetto remembers:

You just got used to people dying. They were dying every day. You saw a corpse in the street and you didn't even look to see if they'd died from sickness or been shot. You didn't even look to see if it was someone you knew. It wasn't you. That got to be all you needed to know.

Falling Numbers

By July 1942, over 100,000 Jewish people had died in the Warsaw Ghetto, mainly from starvation and disease. Despite a death rate of 300 to 400 a day, there were still about 380,000 left alive, although many of them were sick or starving. The Nazis, however, had already decided in January 1942 that their policy of starvation and brutality in ghettos and **camps** was not solving the "Jewish Problem" fast enough. They wanted their lands *Judenfrei*—"Jew Free"—sooner rather than later. They built **death camps** to kill Jews in large numbers and began to send Jews to them. We know this now, but at the time, there were only rumors about these camps.

Deportations

In July 1942, the Nazis told the Warsaw *Judenrat* that its people were to be **resettled** on farmland in the east, to make Warsaw *Judenfrei*. They told Czerniakow to provide 7,000 "non-productive" Jews a day for resettlement. The fact that they wanted babies, the old, the sick, and other unhealthy workers made resettlement unlikely. Czerniakow asked how long this would continue and was told: "Seven days a week, until the end." Czerniakow, suspecting what was going on, killed himself rather than send more people to their death. The *Judenrat*, however, carried on cooperating. Between July 22 and September 21, about 366,000 Jews from Warsaw were **deported** to Treblinka death camp and killed.

A Ghetto Army

The *Judenrat* argued that resistance was foolish. How could they hope to defeat the German army? After the **deportations,** there were only about 70,000 **Jews** left in the **ghetto.** Most of them were sick and starving, and they had few weapons. By the end of July 1942, however, it was clear to many people that they were going to be killed anyway. About 1,000 men and boys formed the Jewish Fighting Organization. Their slogan was: "Brothers, don't die in silence. Let's fight!" They wanted to die fighting, killing as many **SS** as they could. They appealed to people to give them weapons and smuggled some in from outside the ghetto.

First Blows

In January 1943, the Jewish Fighting Organization began to fight back. They shot **Nazis** who were rounding up people to deport. In four days, twenty SS members were killed and 50 more were injured. This had two effects. First, the SS left the ghetto alone, staying outside. Second, Polish resistance workers, seeing the Jews fighting, began to smuggle in more weapons and ammunition. With the SS gone, more people were willing to join up. They split into groups and began to tunnel between the cellars of houses so that they could move around most of the ghetto without ever going onto the street. They knew that the SS would be back.

Fighting in the Ghetto

This SS photo shows Nazi troops in the ghetto during the revolt. The large gun they are manning has been used to bombard the building in front of them. The Nazis shelled buildings heavily and then allowed the fires caused by the shelling to burn out before they tried to go into the buildings.

Getting Out Before the End

On April 20, Walther Toebbens, a factory owner employing about 10,000 ghetto workers, offered them escape—to work in factories further east in Poland. This photo shows some of his workers going to the station. They did work at his new factories for a while, but between November 2 and 5, 1942, all 22,000 of the Jewish workers in the eastern factories, from Warsaw and elsewhere, were sent to Treblinka and killed.

The SS Return

At 2 A.M. on the morning of April 19, 1943, the SS returned, commanded by Jürgen Stroop. They came to "liquidate" the ghetto—close it down and deport everyone in it to Treblinka. They expected to clear the ghetto in three or four days. Zivia Lubetkin, one of the resisters, remembers:

> *Even though we were prepared, had even prayed for this moment, we turned pale. We felt both joy and fear. But we sat on our emotion and reached for our guns.*

An Easy Victory?

Stroop and the SS did not have the easy victory they had been expecting. They were attacked from building after building, without being able to see their attackers. They left the ghetto to make a new plan. Stroop decided that marching in was too dangerous; any building could hide snipers, or be booby-trapped. He decided the safest way to take over the ghetto was to move through it street by street, destroying the buildings from a distance first.

They would start by bombarding the buildings with artillery. Then they would set the ruins on fire with flame throwers. Anyone running from a building would be machine-gunned down. Only then would the soldiers move in to pick off any survivors.

Unevenly Matched

- The SS had 3,200 troops. There were about 1,200 members of the Jewish Fighting Organization and others who were determined to fight.
- The Nazis had 135 machine guns; the Jewish resistance fighters had just two.
- The Nazis had 1,358 rifles; the resistance had fifteen.
- The Nazis had tanks and heavy artillery; the Jews had none.
- The Nazis had a huge supply of ammunition and hand grenades. The resistance had some hand grenades and also some homemade gasoline bombs.

The New Plan

Stroop and the **SS** went back into the **ghetto** and put the new plan into action. The SS destroyed all of the buildings, killing anyone who might be a member of the resistance. Indeed, they killed many people who were clearly not members of the resistance. On April 20, 1943, they broke into the hospital, killed all of the sick and as many doctors and nurses as they could find. They then set fire to the building.

As they worked through the ghetto, burning building after building, the SS rounded up people who surrendered and marched them to the central square until they had collected enough to send a trainload to Treblinka.

The Last Days

The **Jewish** resisters held out for a month. On May 8, the SS troops reached Mila Street, where the Jewish Fighting Organization was based. They filled the building with gas. Some of the fighters escaped through the tunnels and sewers; most died in the gas attack. Among them was their leader, Mordecai Anielewicz, whose last letter to a friend said:

> *Peace be with you, my dear friend. Who knows when we shall meet again? My life's dream has come true: Jews are defending themselves in the ghetto. I have seen the magnificent, heroic struggle of the Jewish fighters.*

The struggle had been heroic, but it was coming to an end.

Captured

This photo, taken by the SS, shows a resister being hauled out of the rubble of a "cleared" building. Most of the people captured in this way were shot at once.

"The Warsaw Ghetto is No More"

The SS finished "cleansing" the ghetto on May 16, 1943. Stroop's final act was to blow up the synagogue. He informed his headquarters: "The Warsaw Ghetto is no more." The **Nazis** played down their losses and tried to present the destruction of the ghetto as a heroic act. Hundreds of SS had been killed, but this loss was presented as "minimal loss of life." About 7,000 Jews, resisters and unarmed people, were killed. About 10,000 more were rounded up and **deported** to be killed. Most died in Treblinka, although some were sent to Majdanek, Poniatow, and Trawniki **camps,** where most were murdered within a month.

Stroop was awarded the Iron Cross, First Class—a medal that was not often awarded to an ordinary soldier. He produced a book about his successful "murder expedition" that included the telegrams he sent, keeping headquarters informed of progress, and photos taken during "clearing."

An Inspiration

The Warsaw Ghetto uprising inspired Hirsh Glick, a poet in the Vilna Ghetto, to write a song that somehow spread around the ghettos and to **partisan** groups. The Nazis had meant the destruction of the Warsaw Ghetto as a warning to Jews and other **occupied** people not to rebel. It may have scared people, but it did not stop resistance. This was true even in Warsaw, where people were most aware of the terrible destruction. On August 1, 1944, the Polish people of Warsaw rose up against the Nazis and were joined by many of the Jews hidden in the city. This uprising, too, was put down. Glick was sent to a **labor camp** and did not survive the **Holocaust,** but his song kept many people going and is still sung. The first verse goes:

Never say that you have reached the very end
Though leaden skies a bitter future may portend
The hour for which we yearned will yet arrive
And our marching step will thunder:
"We survive!"

Timeline

1933

January 30	Adolf Hitler comes to power in Germany as Chancellor.
February 27	A fire breaks out at the *Reichstag*, the German Parliament. The **Nazis** blame the **Communists** and produce a Dutch communist who confesses.
February 28	Hitler persuades German President Hindenburg to pass a decree, "For the Protection of the People and the State," which allows for the creation of **concentration camps.**
March 5	New elections are held. The Nazis win easily with intimidation.
March 17	The **SS** (short for "*Schutzstaffel*," security staff) is set up as Hitler's bodyguard.
March 21	Dachau, the first Nazi concentration camp, is set up. Concentration camps and **labor camps** are set up steadily after this.
April 1	**Jewish** stores in Berlin are boycotted.
April 7	Jewish government employees, including civil servants, teachers, and professors, lose their jobs.
April 24–25	People with Jewish names are not allowed to use them when sending telegrams.
April 26	The **Gestapo**—Nazi secret police force—is set up.
May 2	Trade unions are banned in Germany.
May 10	Books written by Jews and Nazi opponents are burned.
July 14	Political parties other than the Nazi Party are banned in Germany.
October	Jews are no longer allowed to work in the media.

1934

March 5	Jewish actors are banned.
April 20	Heinrich Himmler is placed in charge of the Gestapo.
June 7	Jewish students are banned from taking exams.
July 20	The SS is no longer under the control of the German army. They swear loyalty to Hitler alone and run their own organization.
August 2	Hitler makes himself *Führer*, sole leader of Germany.

1935

September 15	The Nuremberg Laws are passed against German Jews.

1936

	Jewish doctors and dentists cannot work in state hospitals. Jews cannot become judges, join the army, or work in the book trade.
March 29	The SS grows to 3,500 men.
June 17	Himmler is placed in charge of all police departments.

1937

	Jewish businesses are **"Aryanized."**
July 16	Buchenwald concentration camp is set up.

1938

March 13	Germany takes over Austria.
August 8	Mauthausen concentration camp is set up.
November 9	*Kristallnacht* takes place. Nazi-led violence against Jews includes burning synagogues and looting Jewish stores and homes.
October 28	The first Jews are **deported** from Poland by the Polish government.
December 1	The *Kindertransports* to Britain begin.

1939

September 1	Germany invades Poland and takes immediate action against Polish Jews.
September 3	Britain and France declare war on Germany.
September 28	Germany and the **Soviet Union** split Poland between them.
November 30	The Soviet Union invades Finland.

1940

February 12	The first Jews are deported from Germany to **ghettos** in Poland.
April 9	Germany invades Denmark and Norway.
April 30	The Lodz Ghetto is set up in Poland.
May 10	Germany invades Belgium, France, Luxembourg, and Holland.
November 15	The Warsaw Ghetto is set up in Poland.

1941

April 6	Germany invades Yugoslavia and Greece.
June 22	Germany invades the Soviet Union and begins killing Jews in large numbers.
October 10	Terezín Ghetto is set up in Czechoslovakia. German and Czech Jews are sent there.
October 28	10,000 Jews are selected and killed in Kovno Ghetto in Lithuania.
December 7	Japan bombs Pearl Harbor.
December 8	The first group of Jews are gassed at Chelmno **death camp** in Poland.
December 11	Germany declares war on the United States.

1942

January 20	The Wannsee Conference is called to discuss the "Final Solution" to the "Jewish Problem."
January 21	The United Partisan Organization, a Jewish resistance group, is set up in the Vilna Ghetto in Lithuania.
March 1	The first deportation of Jews to Sobibor death camp in Poland takes place.
March 17	The first deportation of Jews to Belzec death camp in Poland takes place.
March 26	The first deportations to Auschwitz-Birkenau and Majdanek death camps take place.
July 22	Daily deportations to Treblinka **camp** in Poland from the Warsaw Ghetto begin.
December 22	Kraków Ghetto revolt takes place.

1943

January 18	Warsaw Ghetto revolt begins.
March 17	Bulgaria refuses to deport Jews.
April 17	Hungary refuses to deport Jews.
April 19	Warsaw Ghetto revolt resumes. The SS moves back into the city.
May 16	Warsaw Ghetto revolt is crushed.
June 11	Himmler orders all remaining ghettos to be emptied and their inhabitants killed.

1944

March 23	The deportation of Greek Jews begins.
April 7	Two Jews escape from Auschwitz and reach Brostalvia in Slovakia. News of the camp can no longer be ignored in the west.
May 15	Mass deportation and gassing of Hungarian Jews begins.
From June	Death marches from camps in front of advancing Soviet troops begin.
June 6	**Allied** troops land in Normandy, France.
June 9	Hannah Senesh goes into Hungary to help Hungarian Jews escape.
August 4	Anne Frank and her family are arrested in Amsterdam.
November 7	Hannah Senesh is executed.

1945

January 17	The final death march from Auschwitz-Birkenau away from the advancing Allied armies takes place.
January 27	Soviet troops reach Auschwitz.
April 11	U.S. troops reach Buchenwald camp.
April 15	British troops reach Belsen camp.
April 29	U.S. troops reach Dachau camp. Russian troops reach Berlin camp.
April 30	Hitler commits suicide in Berlin.
May 5	U.S. troops reach Mauthausen camp.
May 7	Germany surrenders to the Allies.
November	The Nuremberg trials of Nazi war criminals begin. The first war criminals are executed in October 1946.

Glossary

Ally country that fought against Nazi Germany in World War II

anti-Semitism being prejudiced against Jewish people

Aryan word used by the Nazis to mean people with northern European ancestors, without any ancestors from what they called "inferior" races, such as Poles, Slavs, or Jews. Aryans were usually blonde, blue-eyed, and sturdy.

black market illegally buying and selling things, such as food, that a government has limited the amounts you can buy

camp *See* concentration camp, death camp, and labor camp.

Communist person who believes that a country should be governed by the people of that country for the good of everyone in it. They believe private property is wrong, including owning a home or business. The state should own everything and run everything, giving the people the things they need.

concentration camp prison camp set up by the Nazis under a special law that meant that the prisoners were never tried and were never given a release date. The Nazis could put anyone in these camps, for any reason or none, for as long as they wanted.

death camp camp set up by the Nazis to murder as many people, most of them Jewish, as quickly and cheaply as possible. Most of the victims were gassed.

deportation being sent away from a place and not allowed to return

deportee person who is sent away from their homes and not allowed to return

displaced persons camp camp set up after World War II for people who had been taken from their homes and countries and separated from their families. Workers in these camps tried to trace families and help people return home.

euthanasia to kill people as painlessly as possible to stop them from suffering. The Nazis used this term to soften the fact that they were actually murdering the sick and disabled.

Foreign Legion French force, famous for not asking about a volunteer's past life, made up mostly of people from other countries

gas chamber large room, often disguised as showers, that the Nazis filled with people. When the room was full, the Nazis pumped gas into it to kill the people inside.

Gestapo secret police set up by the Nazis in 1933

ghetto area of a town or city, walled or fenced off from the rest of the city, where Jewish people were forced to live

Holocaust huge destruction or sacrifice. When it appears with a capital "H," it refers to the deliberate attempt by the Nazi government in Germany to destroy all of the Jewish people in their power.

informer person who tells one group of people what their opponents are planning

Jew (Jewish) someone who follows the Jewish faith. The Nazis also called people Jews if they had Jewish ancestors, even if they had changed their faith.

kapo prisoner who is put in charge of other prisoners when they are working

labor camp camp set up by the Nazis that was a prison that used the prisoners as cheap labor

liberated used in this book to mean a place, especially a concentration camp, being freed from the control of the SS. Camps were liberated by Allied soldiers.

menorah seven- or nine-branched candlestick used in the Jewish religious festival Hanukkah

Nazi member of the Nazi party. Nazi is short for *Nationalsozialistische Deutsche Arbeiterpartei,* the National Socialist German Workers' Party.

occupied used in this book to mean a country that has been captured by Germany and is ruled by Nazis supported by the German army

papers used in this book to mean all the different documents needed under Nazi rule: identity card, work permit, travel permit, Aryan certificate, and so on

partisan someone who fights an army that has invaded and taken over their country

Quaker Protestant religious group that believes in simple religious services, care of others, and non-violence

race group of people with the same ancestors

ration to limit the amount of a thing that any one person can have in a set period of time. For example, during World War II, food was rationed and people were only allowed a certain amount of bread, fat, meat, and other foodstuffs each week.

refugee someone fleeing the place they live, usually in fear of their lives

Reich empire. *See* Third Reich.

resettlement taking people away from one place and making them settle somewhere else. Jewish people who were moved to the ghettos and then to the camps by the Nazis were promised they would be "resettled" in the east.

roll call count of all prisoners in a camp, usually morning and evening

sabotage to deliberately damage something so it will not work

SOE (short for "Special Operations Executive") group set up in Britain that trained people to become secret agents in countries occupied by the Nazis

Soviet belonging to the Soviet Union; when combined with "Union," another name for Russia

SS (short for *Schutzstaffel)* security staff. The SS began as Hitler's personal bodyguard. Later, they ran concentration camps and death camps. Everyone in the SS swore loyalty to Hitler, rather than Germany.

Third Reich "the third empire." The Nazis saw their rule as the third German empire, with Hitler as the emperor, or *Führer.*

transit camp camp where people were imprisoned temporarily before being sent somewhere else

transport used in this book to refer to a trainload of people being sent to the camps

Further Reading

Frank, Anne. *Diary of a Young Girl.* Columbus, Ohio: Prentice Hall, 1993.

Shuter, Jane. *Auschwitz.* Chicago: Heinemann Library, 1999.

Tames, Richard. *Anne Frank.* Chicago: Heinemann Library, 1998.

Tames, Richard. *Adolf Hitler.* Chicago: Heinemann Library, 1998.

Whittock, Martyn. *Hitler & National Socialism.* Chicago: Heinemann Library, 1996.

Wiesel, Elie. *Night.* New York: Bantam Books, 1982.

Willoughby, Susan. *The Holocaust.* Chicago: Heinemann Library, 2000.

Sources

The author and publisher gratefully acknowledge the publications from which written sources in this book are drawn. In some cases, the wording or sentence structure has been simplified to make the material appropriate for a school readership.

Anne Frank House: A Museum with a Story. Amsterdam, the Netherlands: Anne Frank House, 2000. (p. 29)

Beon, Yves. *Planet Dora: A Memoir of the Holocaust and the Birth of the Space Age.* Boulder, Colo.: Westview Press, 1997. (p. 19)

Bielenberg, Christabel. *The Past is Myself.* Minneapolis: Irish Books & Media, Incorporated, 1982. (p. 30)

Dwork, Deborah and Robert Jan van Pelt. *Auschwitz: 1270 to Present.* Scranton, Penn.: W. W. Norton & Company, 1996. (p. 18)

Engelmann, Bernt. *In Hitler's Germany.* Westminster, Md.: Schocken Books, Incorporated, 1988. (pp. 30–31)

Gibbon, Constantine Fritz and Krystyna Michalik (translators). *KL Auschwitz Seen by the SS.* Oswiecim, Poland: Auschwitz Birkenau State Museum, 1998. (p. 20)

Gilbert, Martin. *The Boys: The Story of 732 Young Concentration Camp Survivors.* New York: Henry Holt & Company, 1997. (pp. 12, 45)

Gilbert, Martin. *Never Again: A History of the Holocaust.* New York: Universe Publishing, 2000. (pp. 15, 47, 49)

Gryn, Hugo. *Chasing Shadows.* East Rutherford, N.J.: Viking Penguin, 2000. (p. 17)

Kagan, Jack and Dov Cohen. *Surviving the Holocaust with the Russian Jewish Partisans.* Portland, Oreg.: Vallentine Mitchell Publishers, 2000. (pp. 14, 32)

Klemperer, Victor. *I Shall Bear Witness: the Diaries of Victor Klemperer.* London: George Weidenfeld and Nicholson, Ltd., 1998. (p. 37)

Laffin, John. *The Man the Nazis Couldn't Catch.* Stroud, UK: Sutton Publishing, Limited, 1997. (p. 35)

Opdyke, Irene Gut. *In My Hands: Memories of a Holocaust Rescuer.* Westminster, Md.: Alfred A. Knopf Books for Young Readers, 1999. (pp. 6, 26–27, 35)

Senesh, Hannah. *Hannah Senesh: Her Life and Diary.* Westminster, Md.: Schocken Books, Incorporated, 1972. (p. 11)

Szpilman, Wladyslaw. *The Pianist: The Extraordinary True Story of One Man's Survival in Warsaw, 1935–1945.* New York: Picador USA, 1999. (p. 44)

Places of Interest and Websites

Florida Holocaust Museum
55 Fifth Street South
St. Petersburg, FL 33701
Visitor information: (727) 820-0100
Website: *http://www.flholocaustmuseum.org*

Holocaust Memorial Center
6602 West Maple Road
West Bloomfield, MI 48322
Visitor information: (248) 661-0840
Website: *http://holocaustcenter.org*

Holocaust Museum Houston
5401 Caroline Street
Houston, TX 77004
Visitor information: (713) 942-8000
Website: *http://www.hmh.org*

Museum of Jewish Heritage: A Living Memorial to the Holocaust
18 First Place
Battery Park City
New York, NY 10004
Visitor information: (212) 509-6130
Website: *http://www.mjhnyc.org*

United States Holocaust Memorial Museum
100 Raoul Wallenberg Place, SW
Washington, D.C. 20024
Visitor information: (202) 488-0400
Website: *http://www.uhmm.org*

Website warning
1. Almost all Holocaust websites have been designed for adult users. They can contain horrifying and upsetting information and pictures.
2. Some people wish to minimize the Holocaust, or even deny that it happened at all. Some of their websites pretend to be delivering unbiased facts and information. To be sure you are getting accurate information, it is always best to use an officially recognized site such as the ones listed on this page.
3. If you plan to visit a Holocaust website, ask an adult to view the site with you.

Disclaimer
All the Internet addresses (URLs) given in this book were valid at the time of going to press. However, due to the dynamic nature of the Internet, some addresses may have changed, or sites may have ceased to exist since publication. While the author and publisher regret any inconvenience this may cause readers, no responsibility for any such changes can be accepted by either the author or the publisher.

Index